James & Cooper

-Adventures-

MOVING

Written by
Fay Harting

Illustrated by
Alice Angel Gan

James and his dog, Cooper, are best friends.
They love adventures and have lots of fun together.
James is always super happy,
and Cooper is always super excited.

James and Cooper are playing in their room.
Mom comes in. "Guys, I have great news!"
"What news?" asks James.

James and Cooper both look
at mom with big eyes.
"We're moving! We're going to
a new house next to a forest!"

James looks a little sad and says,
"But I like this house and all my friends here."
Mom comforts him, "The new place is also very nice, and there is
a lot of space for you and Cooper to have new adventures."

James and Cooper must go to sleep.

Pssst... James whispers to Cooper,

"I think I am a little scared to move into the new house. What if my new room isn't so nice? What if I don't like the new place?"

"New things can be a little scarry sometimes, and that's okay." Cooper says.

"But it can also be a lot of fun! Imagine getting a great new room and meeting new friends who are just as cool as we are. It's like a big adventure."

It's all going to be okay.

Cooper gives James a big, drooling lick across his face.

They can't believe their eyes! They see a large moving van outside the window. Mom and dad are already packing.
James and Cooper wake up to a sunny day.
FRA

James and Cooper start packing their toys.
James packs his favorite toy, 'Huggy.'

Cooper puts his bone in the moving box.
The most important things are packed now.

James and Cooper arrive at their new home. They immediately jump out of the car. They see a beautiful house with lots of space to play.

"COme on, James, let's go explore!"
Cooper says excitedly.

Cooper is jumping up and down
like a bouncing ball.

James is not feeling sure yet.
He waits and then thinks that
maybe this new place can be
a lot of fun. He runs after
Cooper to go explore.

James and Cooper are chasing butterflies.
They enter the forest and start following
winding paths. They step over a small, wobbly
wooden bridge further into the forest.

They find wonderful places
everywhere:
a cave with a view hanging bats,

a small waterfall, and
they see beautiful fish
swimming in a stream.

Cooper starts drinking
from the stream and ...

nearly swallows
a fish!

James and Cooper then come across a family of bunnies.
A little bunny comes up to them, saying, "Hi, I'm Sam.
These are my siblings. Shall we play together?"

They happily jump and run around together until they fall over.
They have lots of fun!

Suddenly, James and Cooper hear someone calling their names in the distance.

It's Mom!

James and Cooper quickly run back home.

James and Cooper must go to sleep.
James tells Cooper,
"I thought it was a little scary to
move at first. I wasn't sure if I would
like this new place."

"James, it's totally okay." Cooper says.
"Sometimes, new things might seem a little scary, but you can think of
them as exciting adventures. Most of the time, new things end up being
a ton of fun. We've already found new places and made new friends."

"So, today's lesson is:
Think of doing something new as an
adventure!"

James gets a big,
drooling lick from
Cooper, and together
they fall asleep.

Find out more fun things about
James & Cooper

jamesandcooper.com
@jamesandcooper
@jamesandcooper.com

First edition 2023
©copyright: Fay Harting
Text: Fay Harting
Illustrations: Alice Angel Gan

ISBN: 978-91-527-8495-2